like their parents.
- how plants and animals change as they grow.

Chapter 4

How Living Things Grow and Change

online
Student Edition
sfsuccessnet.com

Discovery Channel School
Student DVD

How do living things grow in different ways?

life cycle

nymph

seed coat

Chapter 4 Vocabulary

life cycle page 106

nymph page 108

seed coat page 114

germinate page 114

seedling page 114

germinate

Germinate means to begin to grow into a young plant.

seedling

99

Explore Which hand do different children use to write?

Materials

paper

crayon

scissors

tape

chart paper

What to Do

1 Trace the hand you use to write.

2 Write your name in the middle. Cut out the hand.

3 **Collect data** Tape your hand to the graph.

Be careful!

Scissors are sharp!

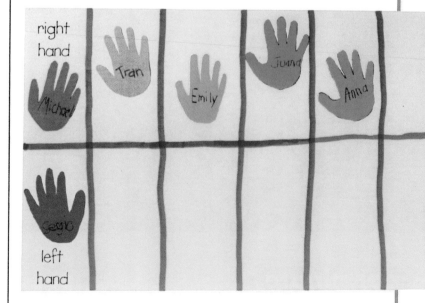

Process Skills

You **infer** when you get ideas from what you know.

Explain Your Results

Infer What does the graph show?

How to Read Science

TARGET SKILL

 Infer

Infer means to use what you know to answer a question.

Science Article

Carol is right-handed. She uses her right hand for writing and to drink from a glass. She uses both hands to button her coat. Ben is left-handed.

Apply It!

Infer Which hand do you think Ben would use to cut paper or throw a ball?

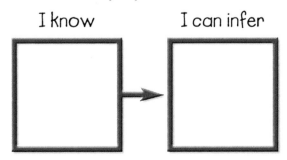

I know   I can infer

Hi Little Turtle!

Sung to the tune of "Itsy Bitsy Spider"

Lyrics by Gerri Brioso & Richard Freitas/The Dovetail Group, Inc.

Look at the sea turtle coming from the sea.
Crawling on the sand, looking right at me.
Hey, little sea turtle, I would like to know,
How did you start out and how did you grow?

How do sea turtles grow and change?

Living things need food and water. Some living things can move on their own. Living things grow and change. Living things can be parents. Plants and animals are living things.

Look at the picture of the sea turtle. The sea turtle is an animal. You will learn how a sea turtle grows and changes.

This toy turtle is a nonliving thing. It does not need food and water. It cannot move on its own. It cannot grow and change. It cannot be a parent.

Sea Turtle Eggs

A sea turtle lives in the ocean. A sea turtle crawls onto a beach to lay eggs. A sea turtle uses its flippers to dig a hole in the sand. It lays eggs in the hole. Then the sea turtle covers the eggs with sand.

Sea turtles can lay lots of eggs at one time.

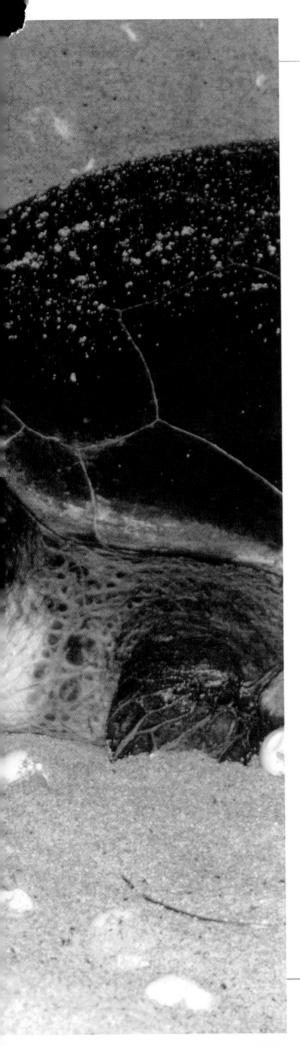

The eggs lay in the sand for about two months. Then the eggs are ready to hatch.

Baby turtles have a special tooth. The tooth helps them break open the egg's shell. Later, the tooth falls out.

A baby sea turtle hatches from its egg.

1. ✓Checkpoint How do baby sea turtles get out of the egg?

2. **Math** in Science Suppose 3 sea turtles each laid 100 eggs. How many eggs were laid all together?

The Life Cycle of a Sea Turtle

The way a living thing grows and changes is called its **life cycle.** Follow the arrows to see the life cycle of a sea turtle.

The sea turtle starts life as an egg.

A young sea turtle comes out of the egg. Young sea turtles look like their parents.

One day, the sea turtle may have young of its own. A new life cycle begins.

✓ Lesson Checkpoint

1. How do sea turtles start life?

2. **Social Studies** in Science Look at a map of the United States. Find some places where sea turtles might lay eggs.

What is the life cycle of a dragonfly?

The life cycles of insects are different from the life cycles of other animals. Many young insects are called **nymphs.** Nymphs look like their parents but they have no wings. Nymphs shed their outside covering many times as they grow.

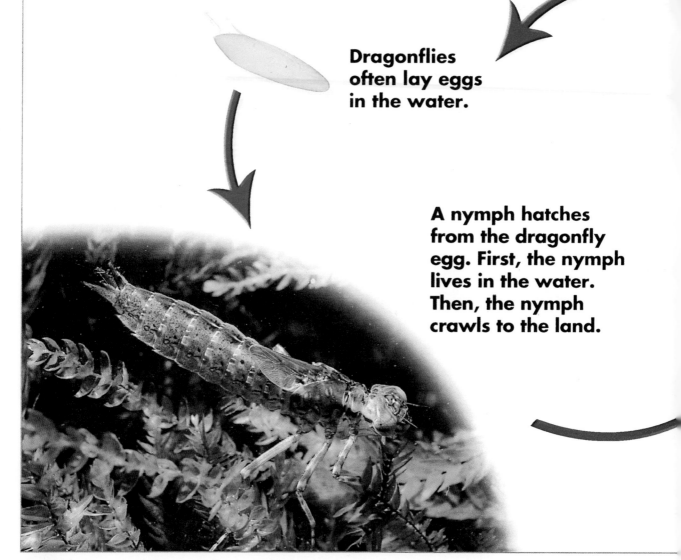

Dragonflies often lay eggs in the water.

A nymph hatches from the dragonfly egg. First, the nymph lives in the water. Then, the nymph crawls to the land.

The nymph has shed its covering one last time. Now it is an adult dragonfly with wings to fly. It may lay eggs.

✓ **Lesson Checkpoint**

1. Tell the stages of a dragonfly life cycle in order.

2. 🎯 **Infer** Why doesn't a nymph need wings?

What is the life cycle of a horse?

A horse is a mammal. Most young mammals grow inside their mothers. Young mammals drink milk from their mother.

A young horse is called a foal.

The foal grows and grows. It looks like its parents.

The foal has become an adult horse. The adult horse is old enough to have foals of its own.

✓ Lesson Checkpoint

1. **Infer** What is food for a foal?

2. **Writing** in Science Tell what you know about the life cycle of a horse.

How are young animals like their parents?

Young animals often look like their parents in shape and color. Yet some young animals look different from their parents.

Young penguins are covered with fuzzy down feathers. The feathers become white and black as the penguin grows.

These kittens all have the same parents. Yet they look different from each other.

Giraffes have brown spots. Each giraffe has its own pattern of spots. No two patterns are the same. The spots on the adult giraffe are darker than the spots on its young.

✓ Lesson Checkpoint

1. How are young penguins different from their parents?

2. **Writing** in Science Tell how you think the kittens are like their parents.

What is the life cycle of a bean plant?

Most plants grow from seeds. A seed has a hard outer covering called a **seed coat.** A seed coat protects the seed.

Each seed contains a tiny plant and stored food. The tiny plant uses the stored food as it grows. A seed that gets enough water and air may **germinate,** or begin to grow. Roots from the germinated seed grow down into the ground. A stem grows up. A seedling grows out of the ground. A **seedling** is a young plant.

Seeds are the beginning of a bean plant life cycle.

The bean seed germinates and starts to grow.

A seedling grows from the seed.

Seed coat

SciLinks Take It to the Net · keyword: seedling
sfsuccessnet.com · code: g2p114

The plant continues to grow. The flowers on an adult plant make seeds. Some seeds from an adult plant will grow into new plants.

The plant continues to grow and change. It becomes an adult.

✓ **Lesson Checkpoint**

1. How does a seed coat help a seed?

2. **Math** in Science A farmer plants 5 rows of bean plants. There are 10 bean plants in each row. How many bean plants did the farmer plant in all? Skip count to find the answer.

How are young plants like their parents?

Young plants are usually like the parent plant in color and shape. Young plants can be different from the parent plant in some ways too.

A young saguaro cactus has the same shape as an adult. It has the same color as an adult.

An adult saguaro cactus has arms.

A young saguaro cactus does not have arms.

These flowers are called foxgloves. Foxgloves grow leaves during their first year of life. They grow flowers during their second year of life. Look at the picture. The foxglove flowers all have the same shape. The foxglove flowers have different colors.

✓ **Lesson Checkpoint**

1. How are the foxgloves alike and different?

2. **Art** in Science   Draw a young saguaro cactus and an old saguaro cactus. Write how they are different.

How do people grow and change?

People are alike in some ways. All people change as they grow. You used to be a baby. You are a child now. You have lost some of your first teeth. You have grown taller. What are some other ways you have changed?

Matías has changed since he was a baby. Now Matías can read and talk.

118

You will keep changing as you get older. You will get taller. You will become a teenager. Later, you will become an adult. Adults keep changing too. Adults do not grow taller. An adult's skin will begin to wrinkle. The color of an adult's hair may change to gray or white.

The members of this family will keep changing.

1. ✓ **Checkpoint** What is one way all people are alike?

2. What are some ways people grow and change?

How People Are Different

People are different in some ways too. Some people are short. Some people are tall. Some people have brown eyes. Some people have blue eyes. People have different hair colors. People have different skin colors.

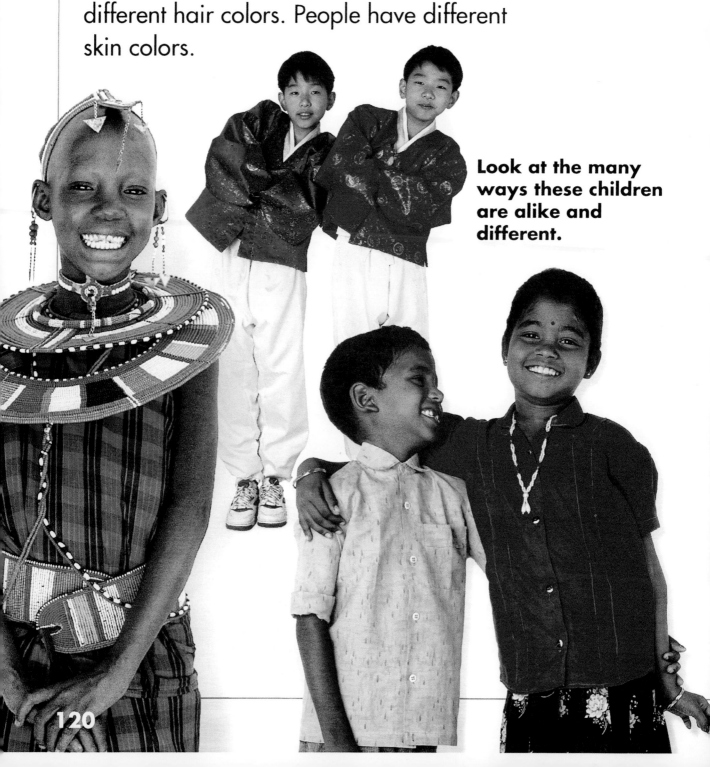

Look at the many ways these children are alike and different.

Children in the same family might look like each other. They might look different from each other too. How might children in the same family look alike? How might they look different?

Parents and their children may look alike in some ways. They may look different in other ways. Look at the family in the picture on this page. How are the children like their parents? How are they different?

People in a family do not look exactly alike.

✓**Lesson Checkpoint**

1. What are some ways people can be different from each other?

2. **Infer** Where did the children in the picture get their dark eyes?

121

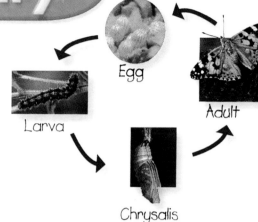

Egg

Larva

Adult

Chrysalis

Investigate How does a caterpillar grow and change?

Living things change as they grow. Some insects look different from their parents.

Materials

caterpillars

butterfly habitat

crayons and markers

What to Do

1 Observe your caterpillars every day. **Collect data** every day for 3 weeks.

Monday
The caterpillars are little. They don't move a lot.

Tuesday
They look the same.
They move a lot.
They are eating.

2 Look for a chrysalis to form. Your teacher will put the chrysalis in the butterfly habitat.

3 Continue to collect data. **Predict** what will happen next.

They're alive! Handle with care.

4 Draw pictures that show how the caterpillars changed.

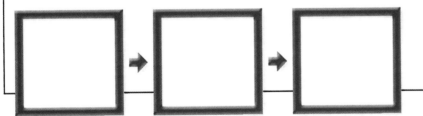

Explain Your Results
1. How did the caterpillars change?
2. **Infer** What happens inside a chrysalis?

Go Further
Can you make a model of how a caterpillar grows and changes? Try it.

Measuring Time

These pictures show the life cycle of a butterfly and the life cycle of a frog. They show the amount of time between each step in the life cycles.

A butterfly life cycle

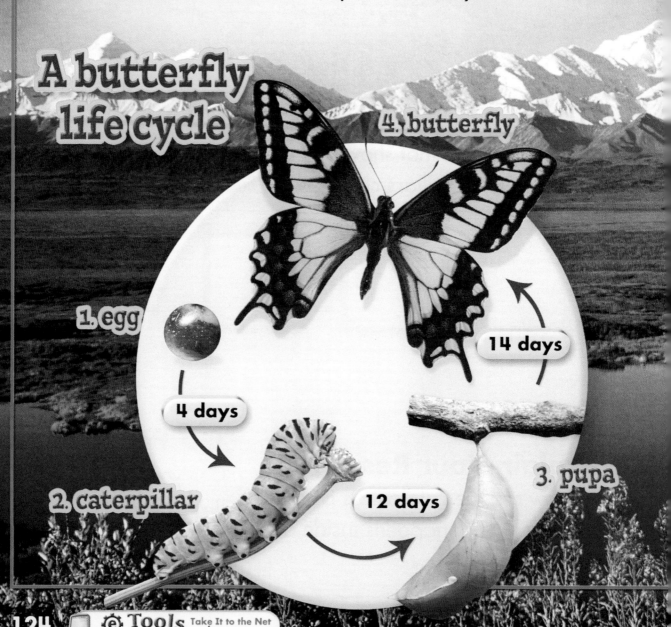

4. butterfly

1. egg

14 days

4 days

2. caterpillar

12 days

3. pupa

e Tools Take It to the Net sfsuccessnet.com

1. How many days does it take a butterfly egg to hatch into a caterpillar?

2. How many days does it take for a butterfly egg to become a butterfly? Write a number sentence.

3. It takes 2 weeks for frog eggs to hatch into tadpoles. How many days is this? Write a number sentence.

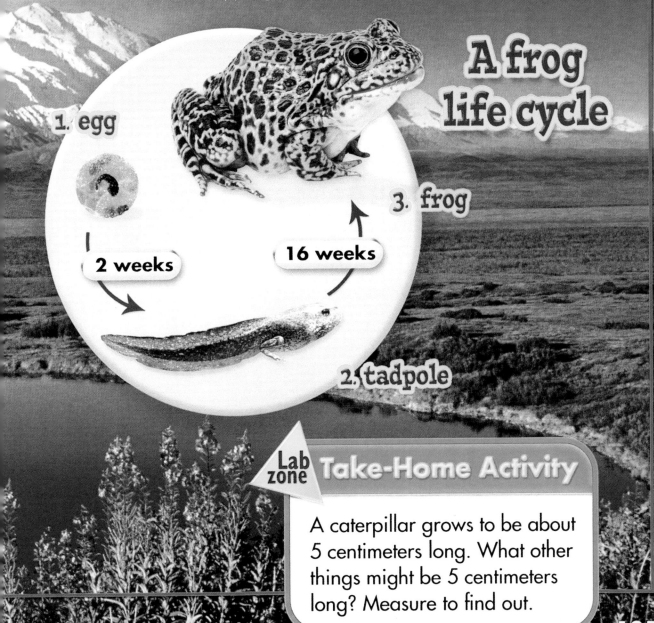

A frog life cycle

1. egg

3. frog

2 weeks

16 weeks

2. tadpole

Lab zone Take-Home Activity

A caterpillar grows to be about 5 centimeters long. What other things might be 5 centimeters long? Measure to find out.

Vocabulary

Which picture goes with each word?

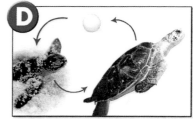

1. seed coat

2. life cycle

3. nymph

4. seedling

What did you learn?

5. How are people alike and different?

6. Compare the life cycles of a dragonfly and a horse. How are they alike and different?

7. What does germinate mean?

8. **Infer** Why does a baby turtle's special tooth fall out after it hatches from the egg?

⊙ Infer

9. People are wearing heavy coats and hats outside. They are wearing gloves and scarves. What can you **infer** about the weather?

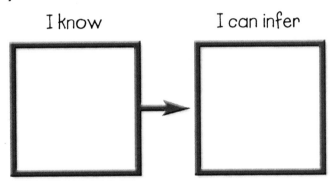

Test Prep

Fill in the circle next to the correct answer.

10. What kind of animal changes from an egg to a nymph?

Ⓐ mammal

Ⓑ insect

Ⓒ reptile

Ⓓ bird

11. **Writing** in Science How might living things be like their parents? Make a list.

SAVE the Sea Turtles

Meet Mario J. Mota

Dr. Mota

Read Together

Dr. Mario Mota is a marine biologist. He works at NASA. Dr. Mota studies turtle biology. He uses some of the tools used on the space shuttle to study the turtles.

Dr. Mota was born in Africa. When Dr. Mota was young, he liked to fish. Dr. Mota always loved the ocean. He knew he wanted to work by the ocean.

Sea turtles lay their eggs on or near the same beach where they hatched. They lay more than 100 eggs in each nest!

Lab zone Take-Home Activity

Baby sea turtles hatch from eggs. Work with your family. Make a list of other animals that hatch from eggs.

Unit A Test Talk

Test-Taking Strategies

▶ Find Important Words
Choose the Right Answer
Use Information from
Text and Graphics
Write Your Answer

Find Important Words

There are important words in science questions. These words help you understand the questions.

Megan lives near a big pond where lots of frogs live. One day, Megan sat on the grass by the pond. She liked watching the frogs. Megan saw one frog sitting very still. The frog's tongue zipped out. It caught a tasty insect to eat.

Read the question.

What is one thing that frogs eat?

   Ⓐ ponds
   Ⓑ sandwiches
   Ⓒ grass
   Ⓓ insects

First, find important words in the question. The most important words are **frogs** and **eat.** Next, find important words in the text that match the important words in the question. Use the words to answer the question.

Unit A Wrap-Up

Chapter 1

How do plants live in their habitats?

- Plants have adaptations that help them live in different environments.

Chapter 2

How are animals different from each other?

- Animals can be put into two groups. One group of animals has backbones. The other group of animals does not have backbones.

Chapter 3

How do living things help each other?

- Living things help each other in different ways. Animals and plants that need each other for food are part of a food chain.

Chapter 4

How do living things grow in different ways?

- Living things have different life cycles. A life cycle is the way a living thing grows and changes. Plants and animals have life cycles.

Performance Assessment

How Can You Sort Animals?

- Cut out pictures of different animals that live on the land, in water, and in the air.

- Put the animals into groups.

- Tell which animals have backbones and which animals do not have backbones.

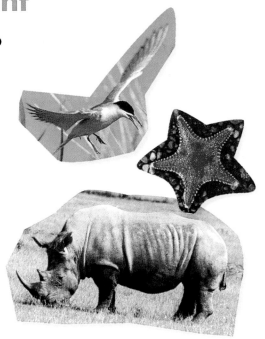

Read More About Life Science!

Look for books like these in your library.

Full Inquiry

heron

cardinal

Experiment Which bird beak can crush seeds?

Look at the heron's beak. Look at the cardinal's beak. How are the beaks alike? How are they different?

Materials

2 clothespins

2 craft sticks

glue

straw pieces

Process Skills

You **control variables** when you change only one thing.

Ask a question.

Which bird uses its beak to crush seeds? **Use models** to learn more.

Make a hypothesis.

Which crushes better, a model of a heron's beak, or a model of a cardinal's beak? Tell what you think.

Plan a fair test.

Be sure to use the same kind of clothespins.

Do your test.

1. Make a model of a heron's beak. Glue 2 craft sticks to a clothespin. Let the glue dry. Use the other clothespin as a model of a cardinal's beak. Use a piece of straw as a model of a seed.

2 Use the heron's beak.
Pick up a seed. Try it again.

3 Use the cardinal's beak.
Pick up a seed. Try it again.

models of seeds

model of a
cardinal's beak

model of a
heron's beak

4 **Observe**. Which beak crushes the seeds?

Collect and record data.

	Did the beak crush the seed? (Circle one for each beak.)	
Heron's beak		
Cardinal's beak		

Tell your conclusion.
Which model crushes a straw?
Infer Which bird uses its beak
to crush seeds?

Go Further
Which beak will
pick up seeds
faster? Try it and
find out.

Little Seeds

by Else Holmelund Minarik

Little seeds we sow in spring,
growing while the robins sing,
give us carrots, peas and beans,
tomatoes, pumpkin, squash and greens.

And we pick them,
one and all,
through the summer,
through the fall.

Winter comes, then spring, and then
little seeds we grow again.

Discovery CHANNEL SCHOOL™ Science Fair Projects

Full Inquiry

Using Scientific Methods
1. Ask a question.
2. Make a hypothesis.
3. Plan a Fair Test.
4. Do your test.
5. Collect and record data.
6. Tell your conclusion.
7. Go further.

Idea 1
Temperature and Seeds

Plan a project. Find out if seeds will grow faster in a warm place or a cold place.

Idea 2
Jumping Insects

Plan a project. Find out if crickets or grasshoppers are better jumpers.

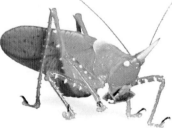